LIBRARIAN ON THE ROOF!

A TRUE STORY

M.G. King

Illustrated by
Stephen Gilpin

Albert Whitman & Company
Chicago, Illinois

To Spencer and Parker, who keep asking when they'll be old enough to climb on the roof.—M.G.K.

In appreciation of Deb Greenwall—a pretty awesome librarian.—S.G.

Library of Congress Cataloging-in-Publication Data

King, M. G. (Miriam Grace), 1968-
Librarian on the roof! : a true story / M.G. King ; illustrated by Stephen Gilpin.
p. cm.
ISBN 978-0-8075-4512-6
1. Dr. Eugene Clark Library—Juvenile literature. 2. Public libraries—Texas—Lockhart—History—20th century—Juvenile literature. 3. Laurell, RoseAleta—Juvenile literature.
I. Gilpin, Stephen. II. Title.
Z733.D757K56 2010
027.4764'33—dc22
2009048126

The design is by Nicholas Tiemersma.

The illustrations are drawn by hand and colored in Photoshop.

For more information about Albert Whitman & Company, please visit our web site at www.albertwhitman.com.

Photo credit page 3: Mike Annas

Librarian on the Roof! is based on the true story of RoseAleta Laurell. This dedicated librarian took to the roof of the Dr. Eugene Clark Library in Lockhart, Texas, on October 16, 2000, in order to raise money for its children's section. She braved a week-long, fifty-foot-high campout in cold, stormy weather to bring national attention to the difficulties librarians often have finding money for library improvements.

The beautiful red brick and limestone library has been a cultural center for the town of Lockhart and Caldwell County since 1899. Below its giant stained glass window stands an inside stage which has hosted many concerts, recitals, and speakers. Famous people have taken their place on this platform, including President William Howard Taft and the opera singer Dorothy Sarnoff, who told her audience, "If you are bored with my performance tonight, you can just reach over and grab a good book to read."

RoseAleta on the library roof.

When Ms. Laurell became the library's director in 1989, she realized that she needed to make some changes to keep up with a community that was growing and changing. She oversaw the careful restoration and expansion of the historic building and brought in resources to meet the needs of Lockhart's Spanish-speaking people. During a time when rural communities struggled to keep up with the nation's digital advances, she pushed to bring computers and free Internet access into the library. She firmly believed that "for many young people, the library serves as their first exposure to books, reading, art, and technology." She was determined to make the Dr. Eugene Clark Library a place where Lockhart's youngest citizens could find all of these things.

The whole town pulled together to make the fund-raising campaign a great success. Elementary school children collected coins, teens organized a car wash, and thousands of citizens dropped bills into coffee cans. When Ms. Laurell came down from the roof after seven days, the town of Lockhart and its supporters had raised almost $40,000, twice her original goal. The library remains a vital center of activity in Lockhart today.

In Lockhart, Texas, stood an old, old library,
the oldest in the whole state.

A hundred years ago, everyone in town visited the Dr. Eugene Clark Library to check out good books and the latest news. Crowds came to hear bands play and schoolchildren sing in front of its giant stained glass window. But over the years, the books grew old and dusty, and people found newer, flashier places to go. The library grew quiet.

One day its creaky doors whooshed open.

"GOOD MORNING!" RoseAleta Laurell, the new librarian, arrived with a clatter of heels on the floor and eyelashes as long as bird feathers. Her laugh rattled the stained glass.

"Shhhhhhh," whispered a library worker. "Don't disturb the readers."

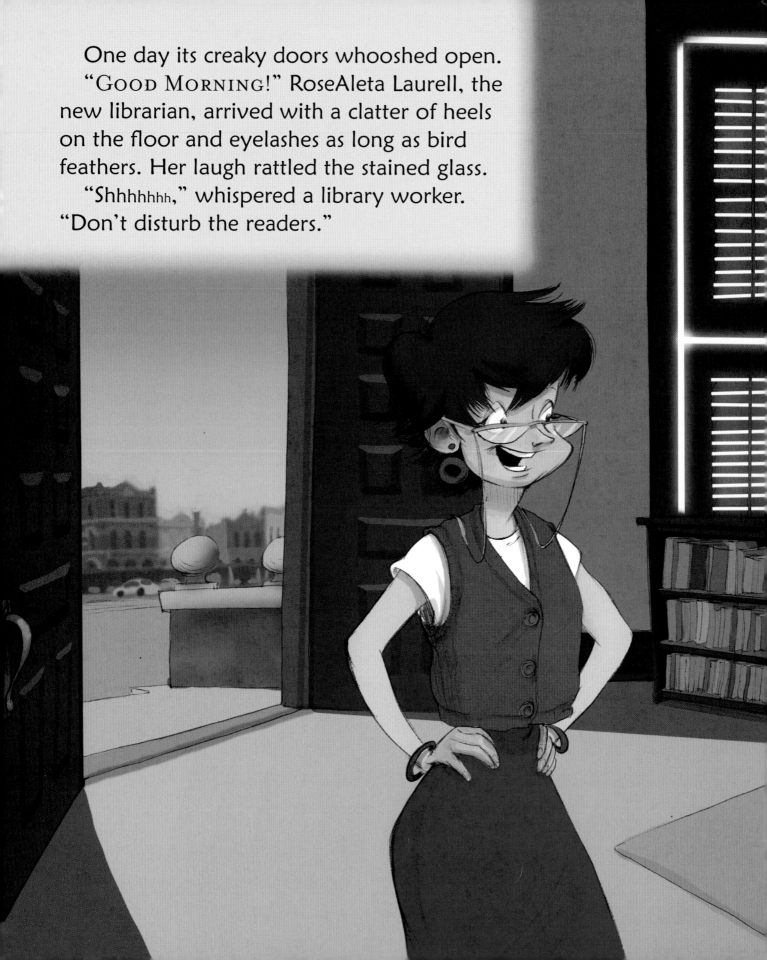

"HORSEFEATHERS! WHAT READERS?"
RoseAleta did NOT whisper.
    The staff looked around, but couldn't
find a reader anywhere.

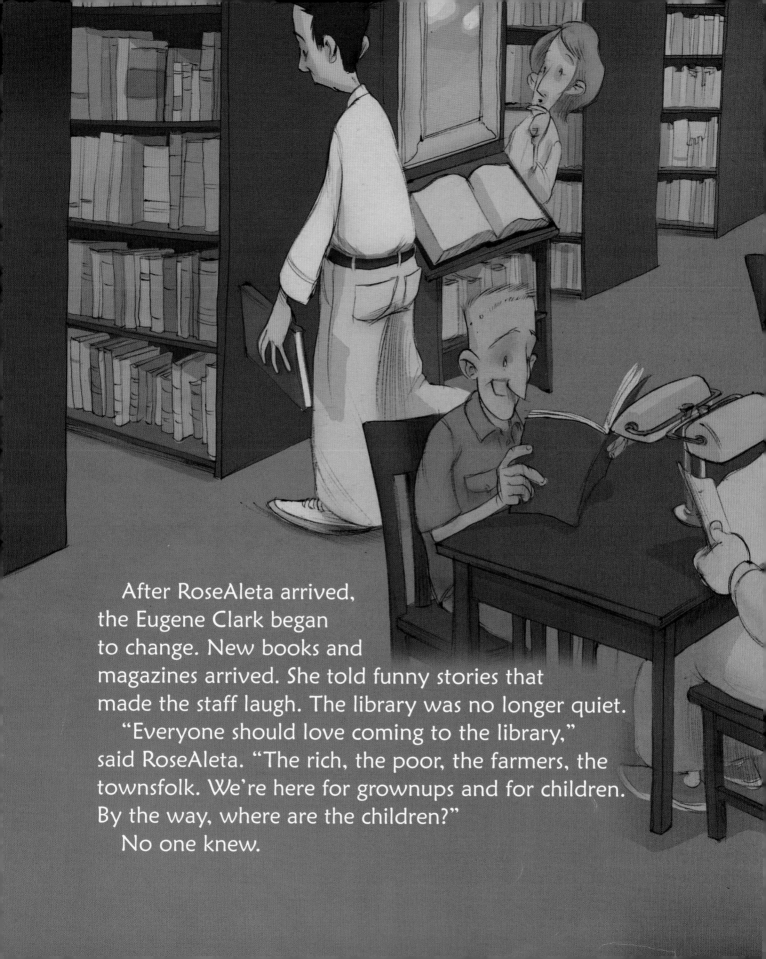

After RoseAleta arrived,
the Eugene Clark began
to change. New books and
magazines arrived. She told funny stories that
made the staff laugh. The library was no longer quiet.

"Everyone should love coming to the library,"
said RoseAleta. "The rich, the poor, the farmers, the
townsfolk. We're here for grownups and for children.
By the way, where are the children?"

No one knew.

That year, RoseAleta planned a Christmas party for the whole town. Wearing the largest hat anyone had ever seen, she led the parade around the square.

"What's on your hat?"
a little girl asked.
"My pet doves," RoseAleta
said. "Come visit them in
the library!"
But after the party,
the children still didn't
come. "The library is for
grownups," they said.

Come
to the
Library!

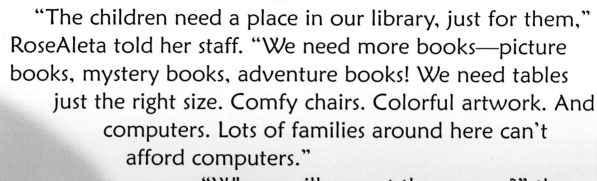

"The children need a place in our library, just for them," RoseAleta told her staff. "We need more books—picture books, mystery books, adventure books! We need tables just the right size. Comfy chairs. Colorful artwork. And computers. Lots of families around here can't afford computers."

"Where will we get the money?" the others asked.

"I'll write letters and ask for donations," said RoseAleta.

RoseAleta wrote plenty of letters to big businesses and important people. But no one sent any money.

"We could have a bake sale," someone suggested.

"We need $20,000, and we won't get it selling cookies," said RoseAleta. "We need the whole town involved. Here's my plan, but I'll need your help."

RoseAleta packed essentials, which included a tent, a bullhorn, a laptop, two cell phones, and a slingshot.

On a Monday morning, the staff stood outside around RoseAleta.

"Be safe, RoseAleta!"

"We'll send you anything you need," they promised.

When people in the street heard where she was going, they had questions.

"How will she sleep? What will she eat?"

"What I want to know," exclaimed one little boy, "is how she's going to go to the bathroom?"

RoseAleta turned to him without batting an eyelash.

"Librarians are very resourceful people," she replied.

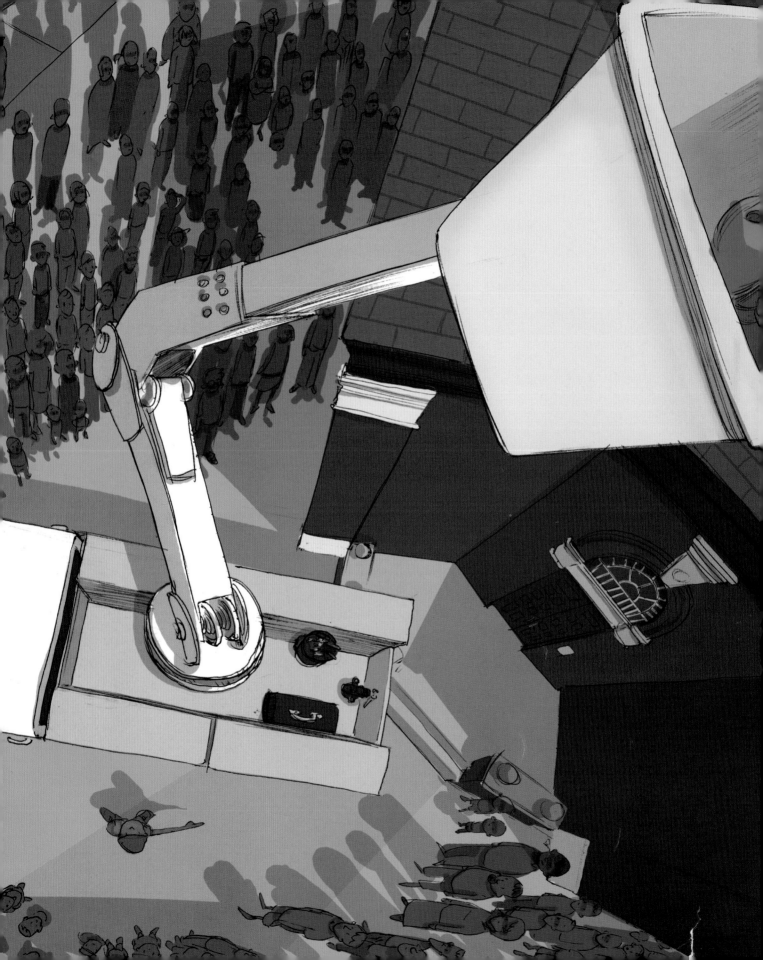

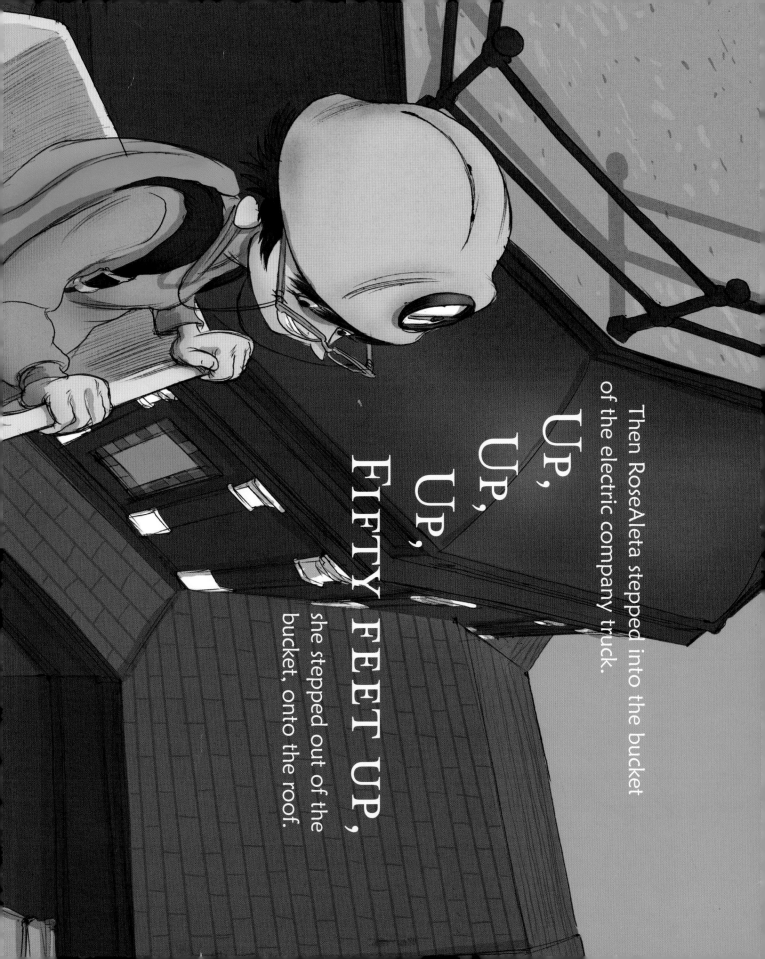

Then RoseAleta stepped into the bucket of the electric company truck.

UP,
UP,
UP,
FIFTY FEET UP,

she stepped out of the bucket, onto the roof.

A city official came by. Startled to find the town librarian on the roof, he shouted, "Ms. Laurell, we pay you to be *inside* the library, not on top of it. What are you doing?"

She pulled out her bullhorn and addressed the gathering crowd.

GRRR

News spread. After school, the children came to see RoseAleta perched there.

"The other librarians never camped on the roof," they said.

RoseAleta launched water balloons with her slingshot while the children danced and played all afternoon on the library steps.

In the evening, she blew them kisses and disappeared inside the tent.

When the staff returned on Tuesday morning, RoseAleta already sat outside, working on her reports. They put her breakfast in a bucket and she pulled it Up, Up, Up, FIFTY FEET UP.

She ate blueberry muffins while the birds sang in the treetops below.

The town official came by again. "RoseAleta, stop this nonsense right now. We are a respectable town. We simply cannot have librarians falling off the roof."

"HORSEFEATHERS! Respectable towns have libraries filled with children." RoseAleta didn't budge.

The high school band played
and the cheerleaders cheered.
Visitors and reporters
arrived from everywhere
to see Lockhart's daring
librarian. The storekeepers
and the hotel owners came to
thank RoseAleta for bringing
them business.

They all left donations.

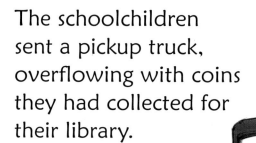

The schoolchildren
sent a pickup truck,
overflowing with coins
they had collected for
their library.

On Wednesday, an employee called RoseAleta's cell phone. "We just got a check for $10,000! Won't you come down?" "Ten thousand dollars is a lot of money, but it's not enough," said RoseAleta. "I never do anything halfway."

On Thursday, the sky clouded over and rain began to fall. RoseAleta grew cold and wet, but she still refused to leave the roof.

On Friday, it poured down harder. The wind tugged the tent lines. The library staff started to worry. They sloshed out the door and stood in puddles up to their shins.

"Please come down," they begged. "It's getting worse."

RoseAleta shook her head and crawled back inside her tent.

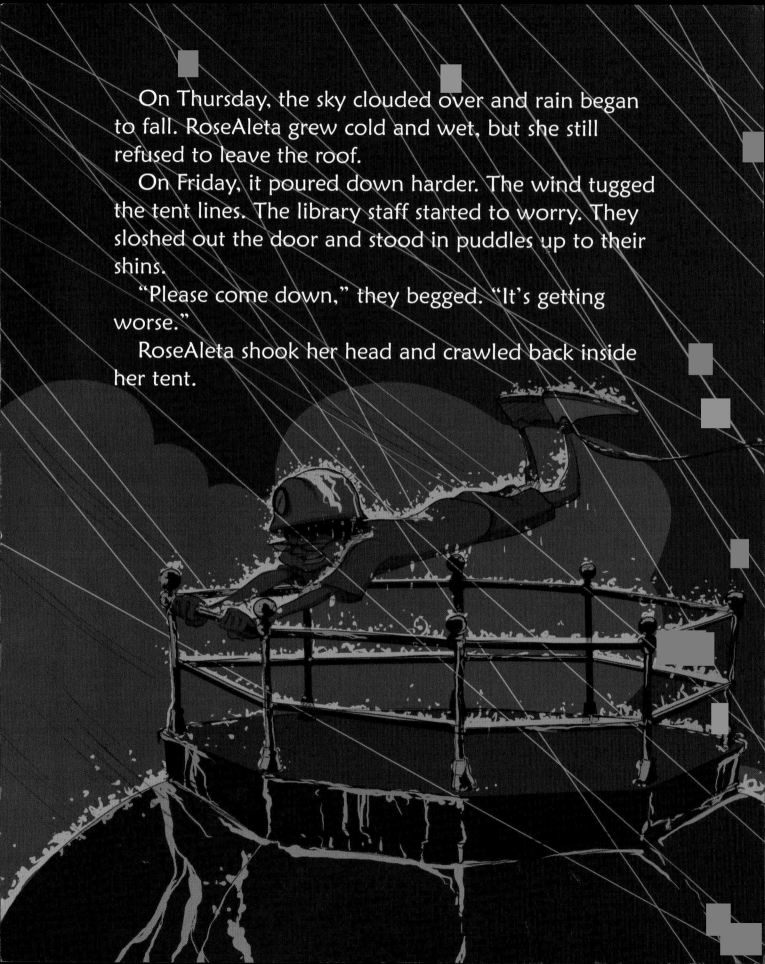

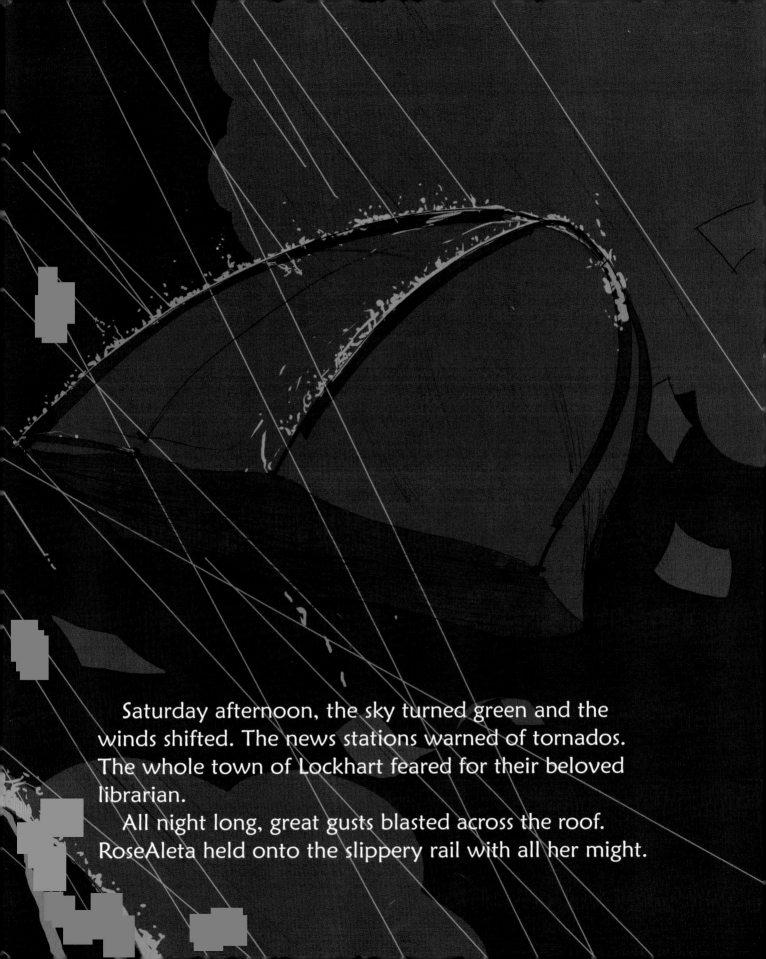

Saturday afternoon, the sky turned green and the winds shifted. The news stations warned of tornados. The whole town of Lockhart feared for their beloved librarian.

All night long, great gusts blasted across the roof. RoseAleta held onto the slippery rail with all her might.

On Sunday morning after the storm, everyone rushed outside.

"RoseAleta, are you still up there?"

"Of course," she said. "A librarian always stays on top of things."

"You did it!" someone yelled. "We have over $39,000—all for the children's area of our library!"

The crowd cheered for RoseAleta.

"You mean we did it," she said.
"THE WHOLE TOWN TOGETHER!"

RoseAleta climbed into the electric company bucket. Her clothes dripped and her eyelashes drooped, but she smiled at all who greeted her on her way back down.

Today if you look through the front window of the Eugene Clark Library, you will see shelves stacked full with children's books and tables and chairs just the right size. You will see artwork on the walls and a row of busy computers.

Best of all, you will always find crowds of children who love to read and learn inside the walls of the oldest library in Texas.

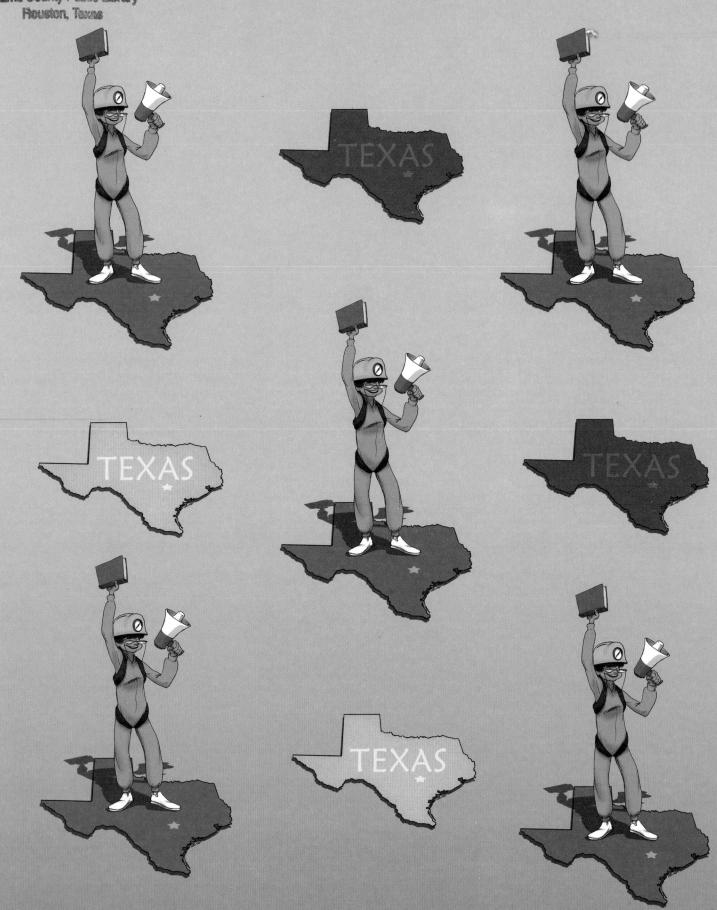